Five Questions to Finding Lasting Peace of Mind and Authentic Happiness

Dr. Armando S. Garcia

Copyright © 2020 Dr. Armando S. Garcia

All rights reserved.

ISBN- 978-1-7342635-3-4

All rights reserved. No part of this publication may be reproduced, distributed, or transmitted in any form or by any means, including photocopying, recording, or other electronic or mechanical methods, without the prior written permission of the publisher, except in the case of brief quotations embodied in critical reviews and certain other noncommercial uses permitted by copyright law.

To

The love of my life,

my wife Sandra

and

to the joys of my life,

my children Arthur and Samantha

Table of Contents

Reality Check 1

How Do You Feel Right Now? 9

Is It Necessary? 33

Are You a Good Person? 45

Can You Be Alone? 59

Who are You? 71

Finding Peace of Mind 81

How to Meditate Effectively 87

Being Happiness 97

Reality Check

(An Introduction)

True happiness is having peace of mind!

That's it! There is nothing else to it. If you presently enjoy enduring peace of mind, then you do not need to read this book, nor any other book on happiness for that matter—and consider yourself fortunate. When you have peace of mind, you naturally enjoy a sense of well-being that psychologists point to in defining happiness. You always know what you need to do because you do not rely on others for your self-worth.

Five Questions to Finding Authentic Happiness

You are motivated by your talents and a clear understanding of yourself.

Your state of happiness may not be something you regularly dwell on, but everything you do, or decide not to do, always concerns a desire for contentment. You may decide, for example, to drink a cup of coffee in the morning because, consciously or not, you feel that it will make you feel better, more content. And the same goes for your choice of career, spouse, friends, place where you live, employment, and the foods you eat. Everything you do always involves your desire for happiness.

Although it would seem easy to determine what makes you happy, most of us most of the time are making the wrong choices. We mistake chasing pleasures and fantasies for true happiness.

In other words, what most of us believe is happiness is just the satisfaction of endless desires. Endless desires can never bring you peace of mind!

There are many books for developing positive attitudes, for letting go of negative ones, and for being successful at getting what you want. But if your happiness depends on getting or becoming anything, then it will not be sustainable. This is because to desire something is already a condition of dissatisfaction, an unhappiness, and even if you get what you want, it will invariably not last.

Wanting something you do not have, or not wanting something you have, will only lead to stress, and more wanting. Even wanting to be happy will cause stress.

But is it possible to live a meaningful life without desire? Does not having desires mean just doing nothing? Not having anything?

The problem is not the desire. The problem is that happiness does not depend on getting what you want.

Most of us believe that if our wishes came true, then we would enjoy happiness ever after. If you get that job, that promotion, the dream house, or win the lottery, then the rest of your life would be apple pie.

Or you may believe that your unhappiness is the result of some drawback, some physical or mental deficiency, that if you could just improve it, then everything would be fine. But the truth is that lasting happiness does not hinge on anything.

Remember the last time you thought, "if I could only get that nice new car, or get that promotion, or buy that house, or get the latest iPhone, etc., then I would be happy." And then, when you finally got your wish, how long did that happiness last?

The truth is that things and accomplishments can only bring you temporary pleasure, satisfaction, or excitement, but not true happiness.

Now, I am not saying, however, that you need to give up your plans and goals for self-improvement, abandon your ambitions, and just sit on your couch and do nothing for the rest of your life. The human mind and spirit thrive on learning, discovering, and creating. It is just that you cannot base lasting happiness on these things.

It also does not mean that you must get rid of everything you enjoy and avoid toxic relationships to find peace of mind. It is not things or people that cause your unhappiness. It is your own mind that is the problem.

Five Questions to Finding Authentic Happiness

I have many things, activities, and relationships which I enjoy. But I am just as happy with them as without them. Things and people, whether good or bad, do not determine nor undermine my happiness.

Happiness is not something you get or become. It is rather what is left over when you do not depend on anything or anyone for your sense of self. Happiness is setting your mind free.

The problem with happiness psychology, and psychology in general, is that it assumes that human behavior is deterministic. That is, that all your behavior is determined by your genes, your upbringing, mysterious subconscious forces, and neurological wiring. Or in other words, that you do not have free will.

Most scientists believe that all you are is a function of your brain. That your brain is like a computer made of neurons that you can just reprogram with the right information. So, they develop scientific studies and perform MRIs to determine which part of the brain make you do what you do.

However, changing your mindset is not like downloading a new application or rebooting your computer. This thinking neglects a whole universe of subjective human awareness that is not accessible through imaging or behavioral studies. It is like trying to figure out how to drive a car by studying the engine—good luck with that!

Real happiness is not about feeling joyful all the time, not even often. Joy is an emotion, like anger, or hatred. Emotions are things you feel, that affect your body as well as your mind as an energy.

Human consciousness is not like anything else in the world. It is free willed and unconditioned. The problem is that we give up this freedom to get a piece of the world. This is the cause of our unhappiness, that we look to the world and others for our self-identity and our sense of meaning.

Happiness is an awareness. It comes from a special kind of understanding which we call wisdom.

This book will show you why real happiness comes from a true understanding of your mind and the nature of human existence. It shows you how to un-condition your mind, how to free up your will power, and gain full control your thoughts, emotions, and your life.

The knowledge and insights of this book come from Existential Buddhism. Years ago, I made a serendipitous discovery that Existential philosophy and Buddhism developed from a fundamental discernment: the Nothingness of consciousness. The Buddha disclosed this understanding in the Not-self Doctrine. Furthermore, I discovered that both disciplines complement each other to a greater comprehension of both. In my book, *An Essay on the Not-self, Nothingness, and Being of Consciousness: A Primer on Existential Buddhism*, I discuss how they come together. This book provides a practical approach to this modern understanding of Buddhism and Existentialism. More in-depth information can be found on my website: Existential-Buddhism.com.

Five Questions to Finding Authentic Happiness

Question #1: How Do You Feel Right Now?

The condition of your body, your emotions, and your thoughts can greatly affect your peace of mind. If you Identify yourself with your body, emotions, and thoughts, then these will determine your happiness. But the truth is that these are objects of your consciousness, that come and go from awareness. Understanding clearly why these objects affect you and learning how to distance your awareness from them, can bring about great peace and contentment.

The Body

Although it is not difficult to notice how a headache or stomachache can affect your concentration, you might not easily be aware of how minor pains, like a muscle ache, hunger, or back strain, can affect your mood. It is therefore important to be mindful of the existence of these discomforts as they can aggravating other stressful situations.

If you take a few minutes throughout your day to focus on the condition of your body, you can identify these discomforts and find relieve. Usually all it takes is an over-the-counter pain medication, a cushion, or a lighter diet to alleviate the unpleasantness and improve your peace of mind. But even if no immediate solution is available, just recognizing the source of irritation is sometimes enough to improve your tolerance.

The mind is immensely powerful. Although the mind and the body are intricately linked, the mind is dominant. It is not unusual to see athletes ignore injuries to finish a performance. We can overcome sleep and hunger to complete a project or obligation. Many people can force their body to put up with significant pain and stress in developing a skill, strength, and endurance.

But the mind can be significantly distressed by the body when we are not paying attention. When you are busy multitasking or hurrying to get things done, a body discomfort can affect you subconsciously, so that you only become aware of your emotional irritation and your impatience.

To gain better control of your body and mind, it is important to clearly understand the mind-body relationship.

We develop in the body, feel its pains and its energy, and feel it as who we are. But how well do you know your body?

If you sit in a quiet place and focus on the immediate sensations of the body, you will easily feel the pressure produced by gravity on the buttocks and soles of your feet. You can be aware the position and movement of an arm or leg or some lower back muscle tension. Perhaps fee the coolness of exposed skin, light feel of clothing, or an itch. You would need to make an effort to be conscious of the movement of your breath or the blinking of your eyes.

However, you will not notice the dynamic beating of your heart 70 times per minute, and the movement of blood from the large arteries to every single microscopic capillary and cell. Unaware of your kidneys filtrating 45 gallons of blood daily and regulating your blood pressure and blood minerals to a decimal of a difference.

You would be insensitive to the digestion and absorption of food by your 25 feet of intestine, the hundreds of chemical reactions occurring in the liver, and the production and regulation of dozens of hormones by glands of your body.

The reality is that we are unconscious of most of our organ systems and ignorant of the vast complex processes that take place for our bodies to survive another day. Furthermore, if you could see your heart or kidney outside your body, you could not recognize them as yours. In other words, you know your own body little more than you know your car.

The body is something that I am conscious of as an object. I can only be aware of things that are outside of my awareness. If the body were what I am, then I could not be aware of it. We will discuss this phenomenon of consciousness in more detail later.

When you identify too much with the body as yourself, you suffer it too much. Then a pain becomes something you fear, that you reject, that you feel you do not deserve. Then, not only do you have to put up with the physical pain, but also with the mental suffering, anxiety, and fear of your failing body.

Five Questions to Finding Authentic Happiness

The body is something that I use to interact with the physical world. If I lose a leg or an arm, I am not any less conscious of my existence, not less a person. The body you had as a child is much different from the body you have as an adult, and the body you will have in old age.

When I experience the body objectively, what happens to it is not as personal. I still need to take medication for pain, or for infection, and take care of my body. I still feel its wear and tiredness. But I also realize that I am more than this body.

In fact, if you are keenly mindful of the body, you come to realize that it only exists in the mind, as a conscious experience. In deep meditation, the body disappears altogether as a conscious object.

When you experience the body objectively, you also develop a deeper appreciation for it. The human body is extremely complex and yet functionally simple. It is a miracle of micro chemical-engineering.

It is astonishing to be able to see things in fine detail, in perspective, and color. The sensitivity of the hearing apparatus will rival the best microprocessor. That the same tactile perception allows to distinguish cotton from metal and minute temperature changes is remarkable. As well as the experience of the many varieties of tastes that come from just four different taste buds.

Although the body is an object of consciousness, and not our true self, it is how we exist and interact in the world. Therefore, it makes much sense to take care of it. An undisciplined and afflicted mind leads to a weak and diseased body and vice a versa.

Getting a good night sleep, of course, is also important for your mental wellbeing. When you are tired, even if you feel you are functioning well, there will be an underlying discomfort which will create mental stress. Your brain will always seek to fulfill the necessary hours of sleep you need for your age, even if it is with micro-sleep episodes—drooping eyes and head nodding. Prolonged sleep deprivation can cause significant stress to the mind and body, and lead to serious accidents.

Keeping a healthy weight and eating a well-balanced diet are fundamental to feeling well mentally. Regular exercise and good hygiene are as essential for the maintenance of your body, as changing the oil and cleaning your car are necessary to keep

Five Questions to Finding Authentic Happiness

it running well and longer. Carrying excess body weight and ignoring good nutrition not only causes physical discomfort but also predispose the body to illness and serious disease.

When you relate to your body as only an object of existence, then you do not suffer its imperfections nor are limited by them. From this perspective, it becomes easier to see your body realistically and make the best of it. Many people criticize and suffer their body, over-emphasizing perceived shortcomings, and under appreciating their strengths. From a more detached point of view, you can develop a relaxed and natural attitude with respect to the amazing body you have been gifted.

Gradually, as you develop your ability to experience your body objectively, as an-other, as just a condition of existence, you gain control over its faculties and afflictions. You also gain a greater appreciation for its amazing powers. The purpose of the following exercises is to help you develop insight into the nature of the mind-body connection. It is one thing to read and understand something and another to really experience it.

Insight exercises:

Sit on an upright chair, with feet touching the floor, and hands on the laps one palm on the other (or in the half-lotus mediation sitting position as described in the chapter on meditation). You do not want to be too comfortable, or too uncomfortable, so that you can focus on your body alertly.

Simply examine and know how your body feels. The pressure caused by gravity on your buttocks and feet, the sensation of the skin caused by your clothing, the ambient temperature. Feel of your arms and legs without moving them. Now, try to identify these as objects of your awareness, as something that you are looking at.

Examine any discomfort you may have, like abdominal pain or muscle ache, as it really feels. Whether it is a burning, pressure-like, or sharp pain, its intensity and location. Try to experience as this an objective discomfort, rather than as my pain. Notice your emotional reaction to any discomfort or pain. Are you are rejecting it or are afraid of it.

Examine objectively the process of eating. How the food feels in the mouth, the movements of the tonged, the biting and swallowing. Be mindful of colors and perspective. Listen to the direction where sounds are coming, the intensity, and sounds of silence.

The Emotions

Emotions are things that you can observe, things that you experience, and as such, are not what you truly are.

However, for most of us, when we encounter emotions, we become them. We usually say, "I am angry," or "I am sad," rather than seeing emotions as things that happen to us. This is because emotions are powerful energies which frequently overwhelm the mind. We become as if possessed by anger and sadness, overwhelmed by joy and fear. It is difficult to notice a sunny day or to dance when consumed by anger or sadness.

Although we experience many emotions, they all stem from a combination of four basic primitive psychological reactions, namely: anger, sadness, joy, and fear. In the same way that the four basic tastes (sour, sweet, salty, and bitter) constitute the wide variety of flavors, the combination of these basic reactions comprise the variety of emotions. Disgust, for example, is a combination of fear and anger. Excitement is a mixture of fear and joy.

The four basic emotional reactions originate from a primitive part of the brain called the *limbic system,* or the paleomammalian cortex. We experience emotions physically because the activity of the limbic system is highly connected with other parts of the brain, nervous system, and the production of hormones. The effect of the emotions is then reflected on the body causing symptoms of chest tightness, sweating, hyperventilation, butterflies in the stomach, headache, tiredness, and many more.

We are thrilled by actors who can portray powerful emotions. It is a great part of what makes movies and television shows entertaining and captivating. Emotions seem to make life more fascinating and meaningful. However, if you pay close attention to your encounter with emotions, you will realize that they are more uncomfortable and troublesome than interesting and meaningful.

Psychologically, the subjective experience of emotions depends on the intention the mind directs towards an object, respectively: grasping for joy, rejection for fear, positive reaction to an obstruction for anger, and negative reaction to an obstruction for sadness. If I create a desire for something—a warm fresh doughnut, for example—and my wish is fulfilled, I feel joy. If I remember that I am watching my weight and resist my urge to eat the doughnut, then I may feel sadness. If a coworker takes the doughnut away to help me with my diet, I will feel anger. If my doctor tells me that doughnuts are making my cholesterol high, then fear.

These primitive emotions are triggered by a subconscious reaction for self-preservation in response to a threat—as they have been for the past thousands of years. The coworker now playing the role of the wolf stealing away the rabbit I caught. It is in this respect that the emotions, which helped us survive the primitive earth, are often excessive for our present existence.

Although our emotions help us to confront the aggressions and frustrations of the world, most of the time what we are fighting or fleeing from is our own mind. Long after an argument has ended, most of us are still fighting the thoughts threatening our self-esteem. In this internal struggle, we increase our blood pressure and release stress hormones, which if prolonged, cause harm to the body.

Five Questions to Finding Authentic Happiness

Emotions have a powerful energy that lingers long after its trigger has faded. The more an emotion is stirred, the longer and stronger will be its effect on the mind. That is why, when someone makes you angry, you continue to lash out at whatever crosses your path. It can leave you in a bad mood for a long time. It is also why sadness can give rise to depression long after the original cause has been forgotten.

Anger, the fire of the mind, fueled by the sympathetic nervous system and the hormone adrenalin, made it possible for us to stand tall against the saber tooth tiger and the ferocious grisly. While there are no tigers and bears threatening our daily existence, anger hurls the same powerful reactions against whatever threatens your sense of self. If anger becomes a habit, then you will be chronically exposed to the toxic effects of adrenaline and excessive stress, causing immunosuppression, hypertension, anxiety, and depression. The truth is that anger is more toxic to the angry person than threatening to others. The more ire we throw at others, the more it builds up in us.

When our intention to grasp or reject an object is frustrated, and we are overwhelmed, we experience sadness. When we judge that threat of injury to our self is too powerful, we retreat, we hide. When the frustration to obtain what we want is too great, then we feel defeated, depressed. Sadness is a retraction of the mind into itself. It becomes weak, dull, helpless. Sadness withdraws our attention from the world. We become absent-minded, unaware of the most beautiful sunny day.

We feel the emotion of joy when a desire or longing is fulfilled. Yet, mixed in with joy is always the fear of loss, and the sadness of knowing that it will not last.

Instead of making life more interesting, our primitive emotions are like too much Tabasco in our soup, or too much sugar in our coffee. They overwhelm the natural flavors life. Emotions are reactions to wanting the world for our Self. At the core of the emotions is fear. Fear of not getting what we want (sadness and anger), and fear of losing what we have (joy and sadness). Emotions will always bring frustration because we cannot find peace of mind desiring a world that is constantly changing.

Emotions happen to us. If we were the owners of our emotions, we would be able control the limbic system and the emotions. But we can see how our emotions can overwhelm us despite our strong opposition. We suffer emotions more when we see them as ours, as who we are.

Five Questions to Finding Authentic Happiness

With Mindfulness, you can realize them as objects of awareness and mitigate much of their energy, and eventually even use them effectively.

Happiness, on the other hand, is not an emotion. Authentic happiness is the wellbeing and peace of mind which comes from understanding the true nature of your Self and of life. It comes from wisdom. This happiness, in contrast to turbulent emotions, is subtle and serene, like a quiet Sunday morning.

When we see someone courageously overcome great adversity, or witness a heroic act, then many of us experience a kind of spiritual joy. This joy is not self-directed, not from a desire of anything. It proceeds from our humanness, from our sense of empathy. It frequently brings us to tears. This feeling is not a primitive emotion, but a transcendent one.

When we can see our emotions as things that happen to us, as our reactions to desires and fears, then they lose much of their power and fascination. They are then not as fearful, not as restraining, not as threatening, and not as appealing.

Be alert to the times when your mind is peaceful, when there are no emotions, to the experience subtle natural happiness of tranquility. Then you will better notice the irritating tension of your emotions.

Insight Exercises:

When sitting in meditation, notice any emotions that emerge. Is it a reaction to a thought or a body sensation. Note its intensity and how it is reflected in the body. Try to isolate the feel of the emotion from the thought it is attached to. Notice how the energy of the emotion lingers long after the thought that triggered it is gone. Notice how the mind feels when an emotion is present, and then when there are no emotions affecting it.

The Mind

Are your thoughts racing? Or is your mind calm? Is it focused or distracted? Are you wide awake and focused? Or are you sleepy and dull?

The reason that we can be aware of our thoughts, that we can think of one thing then another, is because there is an awareness that is aware of thoughts. Thoughts occur one after the other as if you were standing on the side of a road watching cars passing. In the same manner that you can be aware of and connect different musical sounds to form a melody, and then form a musical composition, your awareness rapidly connects individual thought moments (the words) into ideas. Otherwise, if the mind were only the thoughts themselves, then you would not be able to distinguish one thought from another. Just as you cannot see passing cars if you are riding in one of them. Therefore, there must be an awareness that is other than thoughts, and ideas, that arise in it.

Animals have understanding but do not have thoughts. They exist only in the moment, reacting to every situation without consideration, without thinking.

In my book, *An Essay on the Not-self, Nothingness, and Being of Consciousness*, I explain in greater detail how the awareness is always a point of view that exists as if at a distance from the objects of consciousness (the thoughts, emotions, and body sensations). But it is easier just to experience this.

If you sit quietly with your eyes closed and attend to your thoughts, you will notice after a while how thoughts come and go in your awareness of them (in your field of consciousness). You are the awareness.

But if you try to experience this *You* that is aware of the thoughts, you will experience only the awareness of thinking. That is, you cannot be aware of your awareness as an object of awareness because you are the awareness. It is just like a lamp that cannot shine on itself, or an eye that cannot see itself. But vision is clearly revealed in the seeing.

And although you might error on what it is that you are thinking, or seeing, you are always absolutely, undoubtably sure that you are aware, that you exist.

Our human awareness is unique in that it is a self-awareness *at the same time* that it is aware of the things of the world. It is a singular, spontaneous reality. It requires mental energy and concentration to focus your attention and to think, or to remember. But it does not take any effort on your part to be conscious, to be aware.

Some experienced meditators can focus their attention on the breathing to a point where all thoughts and body perceptions have vanished, and they are left with only the pure awareness of awareness. Now, if the awareness were the thoughts, then this would not be possible.

The problem with our thoughts and ideas is that we grasp them as a self-identity, as who we truly are, and more often than not, as an unhealthy ego. We develop into individual human beings by means of a self-identity. This is how we come to know that we exist, how we function in the world, and how we relate to each other. However, if we create a self-identity, an ego, that is not wholesome, not healthy, then it causes suffering. Our own unexamined thoughts and prejudices can become our worst enemy.

You not only grasp, hold on to, the thoughts you bring up in mind, you become them for the time they exist in the mind. The more you entertain thoughts and emotions, the more they become your sense of being, your identity, your ego. This means that if you have frequent angry thoughts, you will grow angrier and identify anger as your normal state of being. Anger is a stressful and troublesome emotion, with many harmful repercussions to your mind and body.

On the contrary, if you frequently maintain good, wholesome thoughts, then your mind becomes increasingly peaceful and pleasant. Therefore, the first step in developing lasting peace of mind is to learn to identify your thoughts and emotions as objects of awareness, then learn to control them and make them wholesome.

Because the mind becomes its thoughts, you also become the thoughts you direct at others. You become the hatred, envy, or discrimination you aim at others, and you become the acceptance, kindness, and love you treat others with.

But even if you do hold positive thoughts in your mind, like kindness and acceptance, as your personal ego, your happiness will still be at risk. This is because even a good ego is made from thoughts, and thoughts tend to change. Life is just too complicated and difficult, and the ego too fragile. Life will frequently frustrate and confuse your self-perception. A wholesome ego will not be able to sustain enduring happiness.

This is the problem with happiness psychology. Even your best ego will be just another idea of who you think you should be. You cannot find peace of mind this way. It will always be a struggle to become something you can never authentically be.

Five Questions to Finding Authentic Happiness

How we mature beyond the ego is what the rest of the four questions are about. For now, it is enough to understand that you are an awareness that is the source of all reality. This awareness is the foundation of authentic happiness.

Thoughts are not the problem. It is natural to think. It is what humans do. Thinking only becomes a problem when it gets out of hand. When we get in the habit of thinking too much and out of control, then the mind becomes stressed and confused. When you identify your thoughts as yourself (as who you are) then there is no way to control them. You cannot see them objectively, as at a distance. You just keep grabbing one after the other until it is time to asleep.

Often, we see ourselves through our past. A lot of mental energy is wasted considering what we wish we had said, or done, or rather not. These long-lasting mental monologues about the past frequently stir up emotions that stress to the mind and the body.

The typical advice is to not live in the past but to stay in the present moment. But is not helpful because, if you think about it, you are always in the present moment. Memories are present thoughts about what happened in the past, and most of the time, very edited by your ego. Yet you regurgitate these emotion-laced thoughts as if they were in the present, like a TV rerun. Difficult memories recur because they have unresolved issues—what we wish we should have said or done. Once you realize they are just other thoughts, then their power is much weakened.

It is good to plan for the future, to be economically and mentally prepared for what may happen, but many of us waste too much mental energy worrying about it. The future is also ideas that we entertain about what may happen, which are typically inaccurate and unrealistic. Worry is fear of situations that usually we have no control over. Worry is a reaction to thoughts. Therefore, once you realize that the future is just thoughts, and not something predestined to happen, then the stress is reduced.

There are many things which we do without thinking, without using mental words. We do not use words to move our arms, walk, eat, or drink. We do not talk to ourselves about putting on shoes, or about how we are driving. We use words to think about things, to make judgements.

We are also aware of our existence without words. We know that we exist. We do not have to think about it. Thinking is what we do, not what we are.

To experience true peace of mind, it is necessary to develop strong mental awareness: to be mindful of the objects of the mind. This creates a kind of distance from our thoughts which gives us the power and freedom to control them. In doing this, we create a wholesome ego that is not vulnerable to the world.

Insight exercises:

Here you want to examine our thoughts. How they appear to the mind. How you bring them out, sustain them in mind, and connect one to another. But specifically, you want to note how the thoughts are objects of the mind, things that come and go in the mind. Then realize yourself as the observer.

It is best to do this as a meditation exercise because thoughts come and go very quickly. As you gain more practice and experience, you will be able to apprehend your thoughts as objects and control them during any activity.

Observe your memories and recognize them as just thoughts, without getting involved with them. Do this also with your worries. Identify and release the emotions connected to thoughts.

Five Questions to Finding Authentic Happiness

Question #2: Is It Necessary?

Everyone knows that there are things we need, like water and food, and things that we want, like soda and potato chips. But often we feel that what we need the things we want. Especially when we are bored or anxious, we may need a flavorful food or drink to help us cope. Many even developed a necessity for electronic equipment.

So, let us begin by really thinking about the things that we need and why.

We certainly need food in the form of a balanced diet. It is important for adults and children to eat at least four servings per day of food containing calcium and vitamin D. The easiest for this is with milk or milk-like product, but other options can be nuts, beans, fortified foods, or in tablet form. All the other vitamins are easy to obtain with a diet containing a variety of fruits, nuts, vegetables, beans, fish, eggs, or meats. We also need to balance our carbohydrate and protein intake to maintain a healthy weight. This is the ideal.

The reality is that, with the wide variety of tasty foods available, it has become difficult to maintain a healthy diet and weight. Advertising is very persuasive in making us believe that we need, and would be much happier, with their good tasting products. Eating strawberries and celery while watching a movie has not caught on as much as popcorn and soda—or at least you never see advertisement to that extent. Along that line, the only liquid we need is water. Any other drink is entertainment.

We need clothing to protect us from the environment, but a brand name does not provide a survival advantage. We want fashionable clothing to attract attention and feed our self-esteem. Whereas comfort is usually not high on the preference list.

We need shelter from the weather, but this does not require a lot of square footage, as we can see from the rising popularity of tiny homes.

Five Questions to Finding Authentic Happiness

We in fact need little, but we want a lot of things because it is fun. We want novelty, excitement, something to live for. Yet, what is driving most of our wants is just boredom!

Entertainment is addicting. The more excitement you experience, the more adrenalin and endorphins you produce, and the more you miss them when the high is over.

Therefore, it is not surprising that despite the many sources of entertainment available, most persons are never satisfied for long. This is because humans have a great capacity for habituation: a decreasing response to a repeated stimulus. It enhances our ability to adapt, which helps us with demanding situations, and it keeps us from getting addicted easily. But it also forces us to keep increasing a stimulus for us to keep enjoying it. Which means that we get bored easily. It is the reason we just cannot have three potato chips.

It is also the reason, if you think about it, why we can never find lasting happiness and peace of mind with the things of the world. The world of entertainment only provides temporary pleasures, and then leaves us hungry for more.

Five Questions to Finding Authentic Happiness

Although it is not front-page news that material things do not bring true happiness, there is still much suffering that is caused by greed these days. Modern happiness psychology studies have determined that once you have enough money to satisfy the basic life necessities, excess wealth does not add significantly to your happiness. Nevertheless, most people believe that greater happiness, comes with increasing wealth, with the capability to satisfy endless desires.

The Buddha identified desire as the fundamental cause of our suffering. He realized that all things are impermanent and therefore unable to bring about lasting satisfaction and contentment. All things include not only the desire for things of the physical world but also our attachment to ideas, emotions, and memories. The more we desire something, the more we are bound to suffer for it.

But why do we desire things to begin with? Why do we look for happiness in the world?

In my book, *Every Drop of Water and Every Grain of Salt on the Way to Authentic Happiness*, I demonstrate, in philosophical detail, why our desires, and our quest for happiness in the world, comes from our existential emptiness:

from the Nothingness of our consciousness. Again, this is easier to experience than to think about.

If you sit in silence with your eyes closed and follow your breathing, eventually, after all thoughts and perceptions disappear, you will experience the Nothingness of the mind. This I also called the Awareness. In meditation it is the experience of being conscious of nothing other than of being conscious. It is a Nothingness because we cannot see (know) what we are as an object of awareness. That is, it is a pure subjectivity.

But this Nothingness only exists if you are looking for yourself as an object, you will see nothing. If you are trying to see what you look like as a physical substance, you will find nothing.

But the one who is looking is more real than anything you can think of!

Because our consciousness is Not any-thing, a Nothingness according to the existential philosopher Jean Paul Sartre, we look for a self-identity in the world. We use the world of thoughts and things to feel as some-thing, to fill our existential emptiness.

This *No-thingness* that we confront in our solitude, as boredom. When our minds are not occupied with anything, then we suddenly realize our existential aloneness, our lack of essential identity. Often this is not obvious, but presents itself as an unnerving sensation, a feeling that we need to be doing something, a sudden loss of self. This is why you can spend our entire life trying to be something or someone, and after you finally achieve our goal, you are nevertheless confronted with the emptiness.

Animals do not have this problem because they are not self-conscious. Their instincts dictate their essence: a lion is a lion, and a cat is a cat. Animals do not have an existential problem, but they are also not free. They are ruled by their instincts. They are condemned to be what they are.

Humans have an essence, but it looks like a Nothingness when you are searching for it in the world. We will see later how our essence as Awareness is our only source of true happiness.

Most of the time, when we feel we need to consume a product or do something, it is because we want to relieve our existential anxiety, rather than for the simple enjoyment of it. It is often a fear of solitude, a fear of aloneness, brought about by the sudden apprehension of the Nothingness, that leads us into temptation. It is the idea of the enjoyment, the fulfilment of the desire, that is most alluring, since the experience itself frequently proves disappointing. It is the thought of dressing up to go dancing and dinning that gets you excited and out of the house. Then you wonder why you paid so much for the food you did not really like, or find you are again nursing a hangover.

The pleasures we experience from the world are ephemeral, and never as impressive as we imagine. You can have a great meal at a restaurant one day, and when you go the next time, the same meal is not as enjoyable. It is fun to go shopping, but the clothes and shoes always looked more interesting on the store shelf. Same goes for everything else, music, movies, literature, food, a new car: pleasures are all short lived. You may experience a sense of well-being when engaged in some activity, like dancing or playing an instrument, or even working, but this feeling will last only until the activity ends. The end of everything will leave us with dissatisfaction and longing for more. But worse than craving is the desire not to have something we have. The mental strain of rejection causes significant psychological pain and suffering.

The good news is that once we stop needing the things we want, we can then genuinely enjoy the things of the world. We can appreciate the beauty of things and people without feeling the need to possess them to be happy. We are satisfied with a simple meal. We enjoy what we have, and do not miss what we lack. We do not need to dress to impress. We value persons for their own sake, and not for the status or entertainment they bestow us. We feel undaunted to offer our affection with no strings attached and genuinely appreciate the affection we receive in return. In other words, once we stop our needing, we can relax and meet the world in a more natural and sincere manner. Then, surprisingly, wonderful things tend to come your way, all on their own.

There is nothing wrong with enjoying the good things of the world, that is a wonderful part of being human. But we need to keep things in perspective. We need to be wise to the fact that pleasures are temporary and not a sustainable source of happiness. You can enjoy your ice cream but not as a treatment for your stress, or with the hope that it will take away your sadness. And neither should you expect that a profession or a relationship will bring happiness ever after.

Five Questions to Finding Authentic Happiness

To have fun, keep good company and laugh with others, to eat delicious food, enjoy music, and to dance are life affirming pleasures. The ability to create beauty is a wondrous mystery of human existence. The word beautiful is derived from the Latin word *bonus*, meaning the good, the virtuous. There is a quality of works done with excellence that is transcendent: as something that resonates within us as spiritual, as beyond the mundane. We can clearly experience this with a masterpiece of music or art. But it is also palpable in all works done with great skill and intellect.

Unfortunately, transcendent works of art are becoming less frequent these days. The modern philosopher Roger Scruton pointed out how the beautiful is being replaced with the hyped-up grotesque and the perverse. These are works of art, music, and literature which celebrate the animality of humans, instead of the transcendent, or spiritual. There is even a greater problem when what we want is harmful. Unwholesome cravings confuse the mind and degrade the spirit.

Life is frequently difficult, and sometimes painful, but we make it much worse when we crave not to have and reject what we do not like. We have medications for pain, for infections, and illnesses, and most of these adversities are bearable and short lasting. The mental aversion to a medical condition, however, will add suffering to the pain that is already there.

Mental suffering can be agonizing, persisting for years unidentified and untreated. Many suffer from unresolved childhood experiences, poor self-esteem, anxieties, loneliness, and many other subclinical conditions which often go unrecognized. Arguments and misunderstandings that have long passed can resurface in the mind regularly for years, causing chronic mental distress and emotional illness. Often the dislike of facial features and body image can be a source of life-long unhappiness. Ironically, all these rejections exist only in the mind as thoughts. It is the struggle against these thoughts that causes the mental pain and suffering.

What causes most of our mental anxiety and stress is our own mental rejection. The stress comes from the mental effort you must make to keep rejecting these thoughts.

When you practice paying careful attention to the body and mind, you will identify the thoughts you are reacting to and deal with these directly, instead of reaching to the world for consolation. You will be aware of what you really need, and what you just want, then adjust your expectations accordingly. You will recognize how heavy and tiring desires and hopes can become. This will bring more peace of mind and happiness to your life than anything else you can wish for.

Insight exercises:

Take time to notice the things that motivate you and determine whether it is a necessity or a want. Are you seeking entertainment because you are bored or sad, or are you indulging yourself just out of thoughtless habit? Is your desire triggered by a commercial or the need to improve your self-image? Focus on how your desires cause mental and physical distress. When not doing anything, or bored, note the urge for things to do. How you feel uncomfortable not doing anything. And, how peaceful it is not having anything to do.

Five Questions to Finding Authentic Happiness

Question # 3: Are You a Good Person?

To be truly happy, you must be a good person not only to others, but first to the most important person in the world, which is yourself. When flight attendants go over the instructions for an emergency landing, they always say to put your oxygen mask on first before that of your child. The same principle applies to goodness and happiness because you cannot bring joy to anyone's life, especially that of your child, if you are feeling miserable.

In *Every Drop of Water and Every Grain of Salt on the Way to Authentic Happiness*, I explain in detail why and how we become our thoughts and intentions. Because our consciousness is not anything, we completely identify with the thoughts about of ourselves and the world. We become our thoughts.

Therefore, if you maintain good thoughts in your mind, then you will feel happy and well. If you are accustomed to harboring negative thoughts and feelings, then you will feel stressed and unhappy. Since we become our thoughts, we also become the thoughts and emotions we project at others. To be angry at someone you first must create anger within yourself, and if you do this often enough, it will become your way of being—an angry person. This is what I call the **Red Rule of Morality:** *that what you do unto others, you have already done unto yourself.*

The Red Rule of Morality is more than a Golden Rule. In industries and hospitals, Red Rules are standards that cannot be broken. The Golden Rule, "do unto others as you would have them do unto you" (Matt. 7:12), depends on your conscience, or a belief in divine or natural retribution, or out of concern for how you yourself might to be treated by others. Therefore, you can entertain the possibility that you can break the Golden Rule, and nothing may happen to you. Especially if the victim of the action is unaware of the harm being done to them.

But, since the mind always becomes its thoughts and intentions, then what you do unto others, you will have already done unto yourself. There is no way of wishing ill unto others without having that thought affect you in some way. It will either immediately make you feel stressed and unhappy, or it will further on, because of your unhealthy mindset, bring about unforeseen personal consequences. For the same reason, every good and wholesome act or thought will make you feel good immediately and will later bring you unforeseen good consequences.

You can test the Red Rule right away with your next negative or positive thought. You will notice the discomfort of the negative thought and the stressful emotions it provokes. You will also notice how light and relaxed your mind feels when you have good thoughts—or even no thought at all.

Memories of arguments we had with family members or others, can linger in the mind for hours at a time and recur for years, without hurting anyone else but ourselves. What keeps us reliving the argument is the unresolved emotions attached to the hurt ego. Since the argument is long past, what you are fighting against is just your thoughts, your memories. If you start thinking about something pleasant, your mind feels light again, relaxed, and filled with good intentions.

Without realizing it, you may spend most your day grasping and rejecting thoughts, and as a result, feeling irritated most of the time. We grasp these thoughts because we see them as our Self, as the person we are. Mindlessly, we become more and more the thoughts that trouble us, unable to understand what is making us miserable, and unable to make it stop. Hating others, we grow hateful. Criticizing, we grow cynical. When you lie and cheat, you become fearful. We become envious when we are insecure and aggressive when afraid. We fight others in our minds without realizing that who we are really struggling against is our own ego.

As already mentioned, if you sit in a quiet place and observe your mind, you can see how a thought comes into mind, then another, and so forth. You, the observer, tie these thoughts together into mental discussions, considering and comparing one to another, like watching cars passing by.

If the thoughts were who you are, then you could not be conscious of them: you would be un-self-conscious. You are the awareness, the one who is observing, the one who is conscious

Five Questions to Finding Authentic Happiness

of your thoughts, and therefore the one who is directly affected by them.

You, the awareness, cause the thoughts you think using your brain. The problem is that most of us are not disciplined in the way we use our thinking machine. You produce thoughts in response to external and internal situations extremely rapidly, often not noticing what you are thinking, and only experiencing the subsequent stress or emotions. Because we are not accustomed to noting these rapid thoughts, many believe their effect is subconscious. However, your thoughts are always conscious. It is just that most of us are not paying enough attention. We are the authors of all our thoughts, emotions, and actions and the owners of their outcome.

It takes many years to learn how to use our arms and legs, as well as our brain to talk and think. But just like we can train our arms to play an instrument, we can also train to be more aware of the thoughts, memories, and emotions. How you do this we will discuss in the chapter on meditation.

When you encounter another person, when you come face to face with another consciousness, you are obligated to respond in some manner. The response will always have some consequence to both persons involved. Even no response will be a response. My actions affect the other, just like those of the other affect me. Even if I ignore someone who sees me, that will bring about some consequence for both.

You do not experience this problem when you encounter a photo, a statue, or a computer. This is because these are only objects in your awareness. We can get lost in thoughts when looking at a photo of someone, but not when that someone is looking at you.

Also, when I confront another person, I become self-aware of myself as being an object for another awareness. I become self-conscious when I see that I am looked at. Things are even more complicated because I am not inherently anything. Since we cannot see our own awareness, we look on others to show us who we are: to give me my Self.

We depend on others so much for our sense of Self, that if it were possible for you to grow up on your own, without others, you would not be self-conscious. You would be like an animal.

Five Questions to Finding Authentic Happiness

We depend on others to know if we are attractive, funny, clever, sociable, good, or bad persons. This is why after seeing ourselves in the mirror, we often ask others how we look.

This becomes a problem, because if I give others the power to define me, then I am also at the mercy of their judgement and goodwill. It is the reason many people turn to clubs, social groups, and gangs in search of identity—and many falling prey to abusers.

As a result, we have a moral mandate, not only to how we make others feel, but also to our own wellbeing. Your words and actions have a powerful effect on others, and strong repercussions to your own mind. Especially with regards to young people, who lack life experience and a stable sense of Self. We must be mindful for our actions and words for the sake of others, and of our thoughts and intentions for our own sake.

On the other hand, because your consciousness is not anything, you are also not confined or condemned to a particular personality, set of genes, or upbringing. Which means that you have total freedom to determine who and what you want to be.

Our condition as a Nothingness is also our unconditioned freedom.

When you free yourself from your thoughts, emotions, and needs, you also free yourself from your dependence on others. You take back from others the power to define you.

By being mindful of what we think and how we act, we correct our past faults. With good thoughts and intentions, we can nourish a wholesome mind.

Negative thoughts are like the salt that you add to a glass of water. Whereas a few grains do not change the taste of the water much, more salt will make it undrinkable, and too much will crystalize. So do our unwholesome thoughts accumulate, increasingly overpowering the mind, eventually irreversibly.

By being kind to others, by maintaining good thoughts, you add water to dilute your store of mental salt. With every "good morning," with every smile, with the attention and importance we give to others, we also water down their mental salt. This encourages others to do the same further on. We all know how it feels, for example, when we get cut off in traffic, how it stirs up anger and frustration, and how uplifting it feels when someone gives us the right way.

Our spirit is moved when we witness acts of selflessness and courage. We cheer for the underdog, the noble hearted, the hero. This is because our humanness is inherently good and noble. This is how we start out as children.

Your personal universe, whether you believe in God, science, or just yourself, is inherently moral. We all naturally want happiness and goodness. True peace of mind and wellbeing can only come from being a good person.

The actual nature of evil is just ignorance: ignorance about who we truly are, and what we really need to be happy. The desire for the world comes from our human-animal nature. It is the will to survive, the will to power, the fear of death, that leads humans to wanton sex, to hate, injure and kill one another. The existential Nothingness gives rise to the unquenchable hunger for the world, causing greed, envy, and addiction.

Even the most unkind and ruthless person wants to be happy, and wills and acts seeking what he/she believes will bring about the satisfaction of needs. The serial killer and the suicide are seeking what they believe will make them happy.

We should, therefore, harbor thoughts of sympathy and pity for those who work ignorantly against their own best interest. And we should punish this ignorance only with the goal of rehabilitation.

True love is to desire what is best for another person. Whether it is a spouse, child, friend, or stranger, true love intends what is best for the loved one. This love is transcendent when unconditioned. All other claims to love is conceit.

To give your affection, care, and body to another selflessly, and receive the same in return, is something that is truly and only human. With the body, we express our most profound devotion and intimacy. A loving relationship, grounded in mutual respect, trust, deep affection, and selfless passion, rises above the Self. It attains authentic intimacy.

Animals are not intimate. They are as naïve in their mating as they are with their aggression. It is all unselfconscious instinct.

The love we feel for our children resonates with the divine. When you genuinely love your child, giving everything and

Five Questions to Finding Authentic Happiness

expecting nothing in return, you touch a mysterious spiritual joy. With our children we have an opportunity to do better, to dilute the salt we have been given or have created. We can become true heroes for our children.

The true love of a friend, or a stranger, reflects our humanity. In true friendship we give each other our respect, interest, and companionship out of the recognition and appreciation of our humanness. When there is no selfish interest involved, when there is no envy or deceit, then friendship is pleasing to the spirit. When we can see beyond the physical features and cultural norms that make us different, when we are kind and receptive out of simple dignity and goodness of heart, then we make the world more human.

If we can understand that the aggression and injury come from ignorance and suffering, then true forgiveness becomes possible. Then it becomes possible to turn the other cheek. Doing this we distil a most pure goodness and receive a most rare and profound happiness. To love someone who sees you as an enemy, is saintly.

Every reasoning human being, no matter how simple of mind, knows the suffering, longing, and joyfulness of existing. This is how we know what others feel. This is what informs our morality.

In *Every Drop of Water and Every Grain of Salt on the Way to Authentic Happiness*, I explain how every human-being is an individual personal universe. The universe, as we know it, exists only in the minds of individual humans. What exists beyond our consciousness is unthinkable. It is the human consciousness which brings everything into existence, in a personal way.

The most important person in your universe is you. You are free and responsible for what you choose to bring into your universe, and you will own your decisions. Because we grow with each other, we know how it feels to suffer, to be respected, and to be happy. Therefore, we have a moral obligation, a rule we cannot break, to ourselves and others, to be a good person.

Insight exercises:

Pay attention to how you react to others and how others react to you. Note that it is difficult not to feel self-conscious when someone is looking at you. Note how this does not happen with a photograph. This is the power of awareness and the meaning of consciousness.

Five Questions to Finding Authentic Happiness

Question #4: Can You Be Alone?

Most humans have a natural aversion to being alone. With the overabundance of television entertainment, movie theaters, social media, restaurants, and many other options for social gathering, you would think that feeling lonely would be a rare thing these days. However, although 80% of adults have a social media account, a survey done by the Cigna insurance company of 20,000 adults across the country found that 54% reported feeling lonely and isolated.

Yes! Humans are social animals. But we seem to go to great lengths, not so much to be social, but as to not be alone. Many people put up with a dysfunctional relationships and abuse to avoid the feeling of loneliness. To drown out the solitude, many keep busy with work, social activities, shopping. When we make some time to ourselves, it is typically to watch a favorite show, read a book, listen to music, or do some other mind distracting activity. Most people cannot be alone for a few minutes without feeling a gnawing urge to do something.

So, why are people so afraid of solitude? And why is this a problem?

For one thing, when the mind is not busy doing something, all kinds of troublesome memories, exaggerated worries, and unfounded fears come forth like ghosts that have been waiting for the night. Then we reject, suppress, or rationalize these consuming thoughts trying to get them to go away. The more negative your life has been, the more powerful, threatening, and numerous these mental ghouls. Some people turn to drugs or alcohol to numb the mind, to find some rest.

We hide from these memories, anxieties, and fears by distracting the mind with entertainment or keeping busy. It takes strong effort to suppress negative thoughts, and even then, they will linger subconsciously, covertly triggering emotions. We must face these intruding phantasms that we have created and handle them effectively if we wish to find peace of mind and lasting happiness. We do this by seeing their true nature and taking away their power.

But even if you do not have troubling thoughts pestering your solitude, even if you have made peace with your past and are not anxious about your future, you will still need to face your Nothingness.

We do not directly experience the Nothingness in our solitude, what most persons encounter is existential boredom. Boredom strikes as a slowly increasing restlessness, a vague emptiness, a meaninglessness. These are symptoms of the disintegration of the Self. You feel as if you do not know who you are or that nothing makes sense. When there is nothing to do, we suddenly experience a widening of the gap between our sense of Self and the world. Suddenly, we find ourselves, as Sartre puts it, "suspended in Nothingness."

The human consciousness is as a Nothingness because it is unlike anything else in the world: because it is pure awareness. Young children do not have a problem with the Nothingness. They simply enjoy existence as it is, without having to be anything. However, as we grow older and are compelled to interact in the world, we are driven to create an identity, a sense of Self. We do this by grasping ideas from our culture, our social situation, our family, and our experiences, and then molding these into a personality. Eventually, we fuse our self-awareness with this worldly Self we have created. Nevertheless, this Self remains a creation, only a series of changing ideas about who we are. So that, if you look deeply in your mind, you will find nothing but an array of thoughts, emotions, and memories, but never anything palpable, or singular, which you can identify as your true Self.

We experience existential emptiness because the Self that we create out of the stuff of the world is always foreign to our true essence. Thus, it can never be fully present to us. It is always an act, always a guise, someone we have learned to be like. We need to keep reinforcing it with our contact with the world, and at the same time, defend it against aggressions. We always need to keep feeding it the world. So that, if you are a writer, then your Self needs book sales. If you are a businessperson, you depend on the approval of your clients. If you are a teacher, you need at a school. If you consider yourself an athlete or entertainer, then you need an audience. Yet, everything that you depend on to define yourself is at risk of changing and throwing you back into emptiness.

Five Questions to Finding Authentic Happiness

People around you function to reflect your existence. The Others make you feel you are a something. They reflect your objectiveness. When you are alone there is no one to reflect this sense of Self back to you, and so your idea of Self begins to dissolve. This dis-integration of yourself leaves you with a sense of meaninglessness, a kind of existential vertigo, that we call boredom.

To avoid the disintegration of the Self, to avoid feeling alone, to keep feeling as someone, many are forced to put up with demanding situations, especially with difficult relationships. It is common for couples to remain together, despite much unhappiness, to avoid being alone. Some parents create a psychological dependency in their children, for them to continue to feel as parents.

If you feel your happiness depends on being with another person, then you are setting yourself up for a great deal of disappointment. Or, to put it another way, if you do not feel fulfilled and happy in your solitude, then you will only find stress and suffering in a relationship. This is because we are complicated beings, with unpredictable desires, expectations, and habits, and with little understanding our own minds, much less that of others.

Frequently couples want to have children to bring more happiness and meaning to the relationship. Not realizing that the financial, emotional, and personal investment required in raising a child well will stress the relationship.

And it gets worse, because not only are we afraid of aloneness, but we also fear our freedom. Since the mind is not anything, since it is pure awareness, it is also unconditioned. This means that it wills with absolute freedom.

Animals are ruled by their instincts. They have no freedom. They must be what they are. Our ability to view our thoughts, and consider our actions, gives us the power to choose.

This freedom is often overwhelming because there is nothing guiding us, nothing controlling us. There is nothing intrinsic that helps us decide what to do. We are free to do anything we want, and this becomes unnerving. Free choice makes us also morally accountable for our decisions.

Evidence to this awesome freedom of mind is the great extent of human moral behavior, ranging from the humblest selflessness to the utmost ruthless cruelty. We have, for example, the heroic compassion of Mother Teresa, and altruism of St. Francis of Assisi (b.1181, d.1226)—born handsome and wealthy, then renounced a life of luxury to become a monk in service of the poor. On the other extreme, there are people like Adolf Hitler, Joseph Stalin, Caligula, and Ted Bundy—to name very few, who showed no sense of remorse, nor limit to their cruelty.

We have moral principles, social laws, and punishments to control our unpredictable and unbridled will power.

Although we can choose freely, for most the will is very much preconditioned. In our project to exist as something, in our craving for the world for our Self, we also become bound and enslaved by it. We carry this Self around as it were a large stone, afraid to put it down.

The Four Noble Truths of Buddhism outline how our suffering comes from craving the world for the sake of a Self. We do this to eclipse the Nothingness, to be something, but in doing so, we sacrifice our freedom. We confine the mind to an idea of Self. We give others the power to define us. We become and belong to have someone tell us who we are, and what we need to do. We create cultures, governments, religions, and social groups to feel some control. We make ourselves safe and sound in a cage.

Your consciousness is not like anything in the physical world, but it is not nothing. You are always conscious, always aware, even when there is nothing to be aware of. Awareness is like a spotlight that shines on the things of the world (including thoughts and emotions) bringing them into existence. When there is nothing to shine on, it is like a spotlight aimed at the night sky. Awareness is presence, existence. It is what you truly are as a being. You transcend the Nothingness when you realize this Awareness.

When we come to terms with the Nothingness, and become comfortable with being solitary and being nobody, then we regain our freedom of mind, and the peace and happiness that comes with it.

Loneliness exists only in your mind. If you think of yourself as alone, unwanted, unloved, abused, or rejected, you become these thoughts. These are just objects in the mind, just paper tigers. When you stop bringing them to mind, you take away their power.

Five Questions to Finding Authentic Happiness

We fear our original freedom like we fear floating in deep water for the first time. You fear not having your thoughts and emotions because you identified them as who you are, as your Self. But you do not have to think of yourself as anything.

It is difficult to be at peace alone if you have a Self to feed. It constantly demands the things of the world for its existence. It is in constant fear of dis-integration.

When you carefully examine your thoughts, beliefs, and customs, you come to understand that these are ideas you use to define your Self. You see that they are limiting, and that they need to be continuously reinforced to exist in mind. Your religious beliefs and values are frequently challenged by the world and by the beliefs and values of others. Your self-identity can change in a moment with the loss of employment, accidents, or divorce. Once you let go of these self-defining ideas, you realize that you were hanging on them for life, just two feet off the ground.

What we learn in our solitude is that our Awareness is a fullness of being. Then you understand that YOU are what gives everything existence.

Five Questions to Finding Authentic Happiness

When we were children, we did not have a career, no personal identification, no sexual anxiety, no mission to accomplish, no worries about the future. We simply enjoyed the mystery and wonder of living the world as it revealed itself to us. We were comfortable and complete with just existing. When you let go your need for the world, you will arrive at this peace of mind we enjoyed as children.

Insight exercise:

To explore your sense of Self in solitude, you need, of course, find a place and some time to be alone. Be alert to the ideas that you associate with your Self. Note that for you to have self-reference you must have thoughts about who you are, about your beliefs, and about how you think others see you.

Note that to create a self-image, you need to recall a mental imagine of what your face and body look like. Or, to put in another way, if you do not think anything about yourself then you really cannot see yourself as anything.

Examine the idea of loneliness, the thoughts that it involves. Realize that you need to think about yourself as being alone, or wanting to be with someone, to feel alone. See if you can experience Awareness. Focus on the sense of just existing, on the fact that you exist.

Carefully observe a beautiful object, like a flower, without thinking anything about it, without saying any words in your mind. Recall your earliest childhood memories and try to remember how it felt just to exist.

Five Questions to Finding Authentic Happiness

Question # 5: Who are You?

It seems an odd question to ask yourself. But, as you might have already noticed, most of us are in the habit of assuming many things. However, your happiness depends entirely on your self-perception, or more exactly, on the perception of your Self. Your search for happiness is fundamentally a quest for your true self.

The quest for our Self usually starts during early adolescence. To this extent, we create an idea of who we want to be and then do everything we can to make this ideal person happy. If it does not work out, we create another Self, and so on.

It is almost impossible to go through adolescence without being asked what you want to be when you grow up. Society, the world, demands that you do something with yourself, that you become someone. As a result, many of us spend the rest of our lives pursuing a true calling. Trying to be that something that will make us feel whole, authentic, and happy as an individual. Most of us eventually settle for a self-identity based on our work, culture, partner, friends, and family, yet never feeling authentically happy, never feeling whole. This is because our ideas about who we are, and what life is about, are based mostly on fantasy.

One of the most common fantasies is parenthood. After we have finally found our soulmate (another fantasy), then we experience a new incompleteness, and are thus moved to create a family. We see the cute baby clothes, tiny shoes, cool strollers, and we develop a deep conviction that happiness means parenthood.

Few realize that rather than bringing a couple closer together, parenthood threatens to tear them apart. Rarely do parents realistically consider and plan on the sleepless nights, worries of illness, and the great demands on time, freedom, and money that come with raising a child well.

When these realities set in, many of us become disappointed and stressed, and unmotivated to make a best effort. This fantasy only eclipses the true beauty and profound sense of fulfilment that come from the selfless devotion of raising a wholesome family.

In the same manner, we hold self-inflicting fantasies regarding our body, our emotions, believes, and our true self. So, let us first take a closer look at who do we think that we are.

The Body

As we discussed at the beginning, we are hardly aware of the body that we feel we are. We move the muscles, but we have limited control of the rest of the body, and no control of most of our organs.

As children, we needed to learn to use the body, and as older adults, we find it increasingly difficult to make it do what we want. The human body consists of 50-60% water, and the rest of the minerals of the earth, or everything that you have eaten since you were born.

The body that you had as a child has mostly changed by the time you are thirty, and even more so by old age. It is not the same body that is growing old, but one that is constantly changing, for the worse. We relate to each other and to earthly existence through the body, but it is more like something we use, not something we are.

If you believe that you are your body, then you will become your body. You become its size and shape, its beauty and ugliness, weakness and strengths, its aging and death. Then you must give in to what others tell you about it because you cannot really see it. When it hurts, you suffer it. You rise with its pleasures and fall with its pains. Your body will never be good enough, and in the end, it will return to nature.

The Emotions

Emotions feel very personal, and we think we would be bored and lifeless without them. Movies would not be remarkably interesting without the drama of emotions. But, if you are mindful of how your emotions come and go, you will notice that anger, sadness, fear, and joy are instead things that happen to us, like a stomachache.

We have a tough time controlling them. It would be great if we could start and stop them at will, but we need things that will turn them on, like movies, and look for distractions to turn them off, like shopping and medications.

We are not our emotions any more than we are a stomachache or the taste of sugar. Emotions are objects of consciousness. The fact is that we can be perfectly happy without them.

The Mind

We discussed that because you are aware of your thoughts then these are necessarily not what you are. Or, conversely, that if you were your thoughts, then you could not be aware of them. In the same manner that you can notice the speed of a car when you are watching it pass by, but not if you are riding in it. Thoughts are mental representations that we use to understand and manipulate the objects of consciousness, to think with, but they are not the thinker.

But then, who is the thinker? Who are you?

The thinker (you and I) is pure awareness, a pure individual subjectivity. You are not any object that you can be aware of (not the thoughts, emotions, or your body). We cannot see (know) what we are any more than we can see our own eye. But we know that we see because we can see things. In the same manner, we know our awareness because we are aware of things.

If you have trouble identifying pure awareness, then ask yourself, "how do I know I exist." It seems like the most obvious question, but the most difficult to answer. If you say, "I think therefore I am," that is not correct because the awareness comes before the thinking (it is "I am therefore I think, eat, laugh, etc."). The answer is that you know that you exist because you know that you exist. It is self-evident. That sense of existing, that awareness of being an individual, is what you are. What I call Awareness.

Almost all animals demonstrate some awareness of their existence and of the environment, but only to the extent of their limited brain function. Humans, however, are the only creatures with self-awareness. Most persons, however, are not aware of their Awareness.

Five Questions to Finding Authentic Happiness

What is commonly understood as self-consciousness is an awareness of the Self (the idea of self-identity) and not the pure awareness of existing that I refer to as Awareness. It is because of this awareness of awareness, that human beings are the only beings with an existential problem. The only beings who question existence, and who know non-existence.

Animals are tethered to the world through their instincts. They have no freedom of choice, no free will. They must be what they are. Conversely, human Beings have absolute freedom of mind. We have instincts but can choose not to obey them. Many overcome our greatest instinct, the fear of death, by risking their lives to save others, or committing suicide.

Most of us are not aware of our Awareness because we are too busy being the world. We identify with our ideas, emotions, and the things of the world to the extent that we become them. The reason for this, as we discussed, is that since we are not anything, since we are a pure subjectivity, we look to the physical world to become something, to exist as something. Although we need to exist as a Self to develop as human beings and function socially, eventually it becomes limiting and a source of suffering.

Five Questions to Finding Authentic Happiness

The Buddha wisely observed that the physical things and the objects of the mind are too impermanent to sustain a stable sense of Self. Eventually, all the structures of the Self will break down under the pressure of change. Therefore, reliance on the world-as-Self will always lead to frustration and suffering.

When we realize our Awareness as separate from the world, then we gain several powers. First, as mentioned, since you are no longer seeking the world for Self-identification, you attain absolute freedom of mind. No longer do you need others to tell you who you are, no longer are you susceptible to the opinion of others. You are not limited or bound by cultural and social norms. Instead, since you are not anything, you are free to be anything you want. You become free to experience and respond to the world in a more authentic way.

Everyone has a learned way of behaving which we acquire from our parents, culture, and society. This is the social language we learn to interact with others. We all have different talents and sensibilities which determine the way we reveal ourselves as persons.

When you release your dependance on the World, you lose need to develop a great personality to get attention. You simply react to others and to situations with fearless spontaneity, with your natural talents.

Instinctively, we sense and disapprove of someone being pretentious (fake). Most people openly accept and appreciate sincerity and authenticity, no matter how untalented.

Another power we gain with emancipated Awareness is self-control. When we can see our thoughts, emotions, and the physical world objectively, we no longer blindly react to situations. We gain a better understanding of our own nature and have more space to reflect on our response. We learn to use our thoughts and emotions effectively and with good intentions, rather than grasping them as ego.

Furthermore, we are no longer dull victims or our desires and impulses. We become immune to manipulation and advertisement. You can easily identify when your feelings and emotions are being triggered or manipulated, and soberly reconsider your needs and wants.

This emancipation of Awareness from dependence on the objects of consciousness (the physical world, thoughts, and emotions) is a Pure Awareness, which the Buddhists call

Five Questions to Finding Authentic Happiness

Enlightenment. When you develop Pure Awareness, you learn to be Mindful. Mindfulness allows you to understand things clearly and realistically.

With Mindfulness, you can catch yourself before grasping ideas and avoid proliferating unimportant trains of thoughts. Your thinking becomes more disciplined and focused. This allows you recognize fantasies.

With freedom of mind, you also gain peace of mind. When you are no longer compelled to please your cravings, the mind settles down. You sense the weight and stress of desire and appreciate the lightness of the unencumbered mind. You find you do not need much to feel satisfied. You experience the same peacefulness sitting quietly at home as at a loud party. You are pleased with a modest home cooked meal. You find that your happiness wells from within, from pure Being, rather than from something you want, or think that you need.

Awareness is elegantly self-evident. You know that you exist, and you know that you are an individual, no proof is needed. Each human life is a personal journey of self-realization, and ultimate transcendence.

Finding Peace of Mind and Happiness

The goal of your journey to authentic happiness is to develop the ability to control your thoughts and emotions so that most of the time you rest in simple awareness. This is what brings you peace of mind. You develop control over your thoughts and emotions, not by suppressing or forcing the mind, but through clear understanding and Mindfulness.

Meaningful, lasting happiness comes from having peace of mind. Simply, when you do not need anything, nor need to be anything, then your mind becomes peaceful. But this peace comes not just from a lack of stress. It is not a "don't worry, be happy" outlook on life. It comes from a profound release of the world from the mind. This peace comes from the realization of pure Awareness. Pure Awareness itself is happiness.

All virtues come from not being selfish, from not being self-bound. Then empathy, courage, good will, moderation, patience, and humility become your natural way of being. As the great philosopher Aristotle noted two thousand years ago, happiness can only come from a virtuous life.

When you have no personal ax to grind, no selfish motivations, then your goals and aspirations arise out of your natural talents and passion. You do not entertain self-defeating ambitions or unrealistic dreams motivated by a desire for fame and fortune.

With peace of mind, your judgement is not clouded by emotions, false ideas, or fantasies. You see clearly what needs to be done and determine the most appropriate response. When you are not having to protect your ego, you do not worry about outcomes. You do your best because you are unafraid of failure.

To know your mind, you must learn to observe what is going on in your mind. The best method for developing this ability was discovered by the Buddha, Sidharta Gautama, who lived in

India about 2500 years ago. The term buddha means the "the one who knows." It is the best psychology because you can examine and learn from your own mind. It took Sidharta many years and heroic effort—coming close to death—to discover the true nature of human consciousness and develop a process for liberating the mind.

Although there are many people who identify themselves as Buddhists, very few understand and practice this teaching as it was originally intended. Both in the east and west, Buddhism is misunderstood as a religion rather than the powerful psychology it really is. Its integration into modern psychology has been limited to the practice of Mindfulness, thus much restricting its effectiveness.

Mindfulness, as presently applied to modern positive psychology, only allows you to identify your negative attitudes and to substitute them with positive ones. Although it has proven effective in promoting a healthier mind, in reducing stress, and improving personal relationships, it cannot by itself bring about enduring peace of mind and happiness.

Mindfulness has been described as of paying attention to the present moment in a nonjudgmental way. Mindfulness is just paying close attention. It is what you do when you are deciding which avocado to buy or looking for an address. The difficult part is in not being judgmental (which is being objective). It is not easy to see your thoughts and emotions dispassionately as avocados.

To truly be nonjudgmental, or detached from your thoughts, you need the wisdom revealed by the Buddha's Not-self Doctrine (Anatta-Lakhana Sutta: The Discourse on the Not-self Characteristic (SN 22.59):

> Bhikkhus, form is not-self. Were form self, then this form would not lead to affliction, and one could have it of form: 'Let my form be thus, let my form be not thus.' And since form is not-self, so it leads to affliction, and none can have it of form: 'Let my form be thus, let my form be not thus.'
>
> Bhikkhus, feeling is not-self...
>
> Bhikkhus, perception is not-self...
>
> Bhikkhus, determinations are not-self...
>
> Bhikkhus, consciousness is not self. Were consciousness self, then this consciousness would not lead to affliction, and one could have it of consciousness: "Let my consciousness be thus, let my

consciousness be not thus." And since consciousness is not-self, so it leads to affliction, and none can have it of consciousness: "Let my consciousness be thus, let my consciousness be not thus."

But to arrive at a realization, to fully comprehend it and make it work for you, you need to practice meditation.

Meditation is just finding a quite space where you can sit and examine your mind for a little while without a lot of distraction. You need to look closely at (be mindful of) the objects of your mind. When you do this, you begin to see how you produce your thoughts and emotions, and how you can use your will power to control them effectively. You begin to see how you react to your thoughts and memories with emotions in defense of your ego, the Self you have created. Meditation is a method of stepping back into your Nothingness, into your absolute subjectivity, so that you do not grasp and react to whatever comes into mind. This is the way to be truly nonjudgmental.

With time, Mindful Meditation will allow to realize that you are more than your physical existence, your thoughts, and your emotions. That you are not the objects of your consciousness (Not-self). That you are pure awareness of existing.

Five Questions to Finding Authentic Happiness

Mindfulness Meditation allows you to see yourself and the things of the world as they truly are, clearly and unbiased, not as you hope or wish they would be, not through fantasies.

This pure awareness of existing is a natural state of peacefulness and happiness. It is the original source of all that is beauty and meaningfulness. It is a realization that the Buddha called Enlightenment.

Enlightenment is not a state of mind you acquire or develop. You do not get to it by becoming anything. it is much simpler than that. It is what is left when you let everything go. When you realize that the Self, which you have created and have been carrying and protecting, is not like your child, but like a heavy stone that you have been carrying around. What you develop with the practice of mediation is non-identification: just a simple awareness.

HOW TO MEDITATE EFFECTIVELY

There are many misconceptions as to the aim of Buddhist meditation. Most of the instructions that you may come across make it much more complicated than it needs to be. Here we will discuss a simple and effective method that will allow you to study your mind. To see how your thoughts come, how they go away, and how they trigger your emotions.

While it is not important how you sit to meditate, you do not want to be either too comfortable or too uncomfortable. For this, it is sufficient to sit upright on a chair, without reclining, with your hands on your thighs. If possible, sit on a floor in the half-lotus yoga position (sitting on a 5-10-inch cushion, with the lower legs folded-in one on top of the other, and the hands resting one on the other in the center). The back should be comfortably straight—without straining. The half-lotus position strikes the right balance between comfort and discomfort and provides a sort of "mood" for what is going to happen. It is like being in a ready position to run a race or waiting to hit a tennis ball. You should experiment until you find your best, somewhat comfortable position.

Once a semi-comfortable sitting position is achieved, then you focus on the general awareness of the breathing. The best object for calming and focusing the mind is *the breathing* because it is readily available, and it is a quite simple process. Following the breathing, you *know* when you are breathing in and *know* when breathing out. You do not need to control the breathing or give it too much importance, just be aware of it, just know it. It is straightforward to know that you are breathing.

If you try to focus on the feeling of the breath on your nose, or abdomen, or diaphragm—like it is often recommend—then it becomes mindfulness of nose, abdomen, or diaphragm. We want to focus on the simple experience of breathing, with the intent of calming the thoughts and emotions, so you can apprehend them as Not-self. Although it is traditionally referred to as concentration meditation, with breathing meditation we strengthen both our ability to concentrate and to be mindful.

Knowing the breathing should be easy and relaxing. Here there is nothing else to do with your awareness than know the breathing and everything else which appears in the mind as an object that you are looking at, as Not-self.

If you have thoughts about plans you are making, about a conversation, or scenes from a movie, you simply know that there are thoughts, recognize their mental object-ness. They will fade away as you return your attention to the breathing. Some persons may experience colored clouds, a white light, or other obscure mental phenomena. These are not omens of anything, just manifestations of a deepening concentration, just more objects that are Not-self.

Anything and everything that you can observe is not you. Everything other than awareness is not your true self.

Any bodily sensation should be also noted as Not-self: as an object of awareness. Unless you have a particular physical ailment, you will notice much more than the sensations of the skin, the pressure of your weight on the buttocks, the position of the legs, or maybe a slight discomfort from the sitting position.

The purpose of mindfulness meditation with regards to the body is to *know* the body as Not-self. To fully realize the perception of the body as object, as distinct from your conscious point of view, as not being your true essence.

Whatever manifests, whether discomfort, an itch, a numbness, this is all seen as Not-self, as just something you are observing, something with a transient existence. Putting up with some discomfort as a test of your endurance is an attachment to an idea. As Gautama the Buddha painfully discovered, there is no purpose or benefit in torturing the body.

With the same understanding, you do not need to be overly concerned with your surroundings. If you try to find a perfectly quiet place to meditate, you will be frustrated in your effort—and if you find it, you might fall asleep. If there is the noise, a dog barking, or a door slamming, then these are just other objects (just sounds) for the mind to observe and not grasp. Any emotional reactions to distractions will only bring more objects to know as Not-self. Whatever comes up in the world, we plainly and mindfully accept as Not-self—nothing else to do.

Five Questions to Finding Authentic Happiness

The more you practice seeing everything as Not-self, the more obvious it will be that the World is other than your awareness of it. The distance from your awareness to the objects of consciousness becomes greater.

Some teachers emphasize what is called Jhana, or absorption, as the principal objective of breathing meditation, or even as a requisite for Enlightenment. Absorption occurs when the mind becomes so profoundly focused on the breathing that all other perceptions disappear, eventually the breathing as well, only remaining an awareness of awareness.

Some Jhana enthusiasts report remaining in this state of suspended animation for hours, some even days, barely breathing and with a minimal pulse. After coming out of Jhana, practitioners usually report feeling a serene joyfulness and a detachment from the world which may last for days. The problem with this experience is that however wonderful it may be, it will not last. Soon the world will return with its problems and demands to darken the illumination, leaving the practitioner yearning for another great trip.

The experience of Jhana, in mild doses, is invaluable in establishing a sense of liberation from the World and in helping to identifying Awareness. But if overemphasized, it will cause attachment and discouragement. So that if you have never attained Jhana then you will feel that you are not making progress and become disheartened. If you have had a blissful experience, then you will be disappointed if it does not recur or yearn for more when you are out of it. Some practitioners may even confuse Jhana with enlightenment, causing confusion and disappointment.

The purpose of mindfulness of breathing, or concentration meditation, is to provide an uninteresting object for the mind to focus on and not get lost grasping whatever pops into the field of awareness. It is like a rudder to steady the mind, not a club to beat down your thoughts. Suppression of the objects of the mind will cause stress and anxiety.

When you first start to practice, you may get bored with the monotony of the breathing and may latch on to any thought, memory, or emotion. With patience, practice, and motivation, however, you will begin to recognize your point of view as a center, and everything else as what is changing around you. Eventually, this center will become peaceful and pleasant. In contrast, you will feel the world outside your awareness tiring and irritating. As the famed Theravada monk Ajahn Cha would say, meditation should be like a peaceful vacation with nothing to worry about, nothing to do.

Nonetheless, initially the breathing may feel heavy and forced, and you may be bothered by itching, throat discomfort, or other bodily sensation. In this case, it helps to observe your breathing and body as if it were that of another person.

Once your attention is unwavering, the breathing will slow down, becoming relaxed and enjoyable. As you identify your thoughts as mental objects and avoid getting involved with them, your awareness will become more adept at staying with the respiration. The thoughts and other mind objects will become less tempting and less frequent. Eventually, the thoughts stop appearing, the mind will relax and settle with the breathing into an awareness of peacefulness. This peacefulness then becomes the new focus of attention.

When all my thoughts stop, I am only aware of my breathing, but it feels as if disembodied, as I have lost contact with all bodily senses. It feels as if it is my mind that it is now barely breathing. I am relaxed and content witnessing the peacefulness of my mind. At this point, I can decide to completely let go the breathing and become totally immersed in the experience of pure awareness (Jhana) or remain within the perspective of Notself. In the former, there is no perspective on anything: I am completely absorbed in the pleasant awareness of pure existing. My consciousness is pure subjectivity. In the latter, I am aware of being pure awareness separated from the objects of consciousness. While both experiences are helpful, it is the experience of Pure Awareness that I can bring back to the mundane world. This experience of Pure Awareness is neither subtle nor obscure, but rather, an immensely powerful awareness of existing. In fact, it is what gives existence to everything.

Once you have become adept at calming the mind and not grasping your thoughts during meditation, then I recommend practicing Nothingness Meditation. Nothingness Meditation entails doing nothing. It is just sitting anywhere for whatever time you have available and attending to nothing but your awareness of existing.

Initially, to develop this awareness, you can ask yourself, "how do I know I exist," until you arrive at the that essential experience of just existing. This practice helps to avoid the grasping of meditation and mindfulness as an identity, as something special you do. Since no special wardrobe or practice hall is needed, it does not impress you as being something that makes you special. It is like Zen meditation but without the trappings and rituals that can make it another attachment.

With Nothing Meditation, you are not following your breath or doing anything special, but simply disregarding anything which comes to mind, any thought, or any urge to do something: all is seen as Not-self and let pass. Your focus is only on the awareness of existing. You just relax and hang out for a while just enjoying your existence.

This is mediation also helps you recognize that urge of the mind to keep occupied, to keep doing something. It is like a mini mental vacation.

I keep my eyes open, gently observing whatever is present, but without elaborating any thoughts about what I see. I do not suppress my thoughts either or focus on my breath intentionally. After a while, you develop an appreciation for the lightness and clarity of pure existing. This in contrast to the heaviness of thoughts, the irritation of emotions, and the exhausting urging after things.

Concentration meditation should not be practiced while doing anything that requires alertness to a situation, like driving, working, or taking care of children. For example, if you are driving, then you should be practicing mindfulness of driving—that is, being very attentive to traffic.

The outcome of mindfulness meditation is a cleansing of the mind. It is purged of the World for a while. During meditation, the mind is peaceful and content, full of itself, resting in Being. Once the World returns, everything is the same except for a change in your perspective. You are as if at a distance from everything. No longer dragged and absorbed by the movement of the world, hardly aware of your own existence. This realization of Being unattached to the world is Enlightenment. It is the beginning of the process of healing. It is peace of mind.

Being Happiness

When you become fully aware that your body, the physical world, your thoughts, and emotions are not-self, then you settle naturally into peacefulness of mind and happiness. This happiness is unshakeable no matter what else is happening. It is authentic because it does not depend on anything or anyone for its existence, nor is it undermined by anything either.

However, this does not mean that you will not have painful experiences. Human existence is mostly about pain and suffering. But suffering is psychological. It is about fearing Self-injury or Self-destruction. Suffering is resistance, non-acceptance, fearfulness. It is this suffering that evaporates with the happiness of just Being.

When you are this happiness, you take things as they come and do what needs to be done. Since you do not depend on anyone for a sense of Self, you accept everyone genuinely, without conditions.

Authentic happiness comes with total freedom of mind. We are enslaved by our desires and fears. Desire is what causes suffering. Even the desire for happiness causes suffering. But desires are a problem when they originate from the Self, when self-directed. For example, when you want to play the piano because you want fame and wealth, rather than from an appreciation and talent for music.

When we fully realize this, we relax our grip and let all things go their own way. Then you are free to enjoy the beauty and pleasures of the world with simplicity, without the need to possess nor demand for more. Everything is enough as it is.

When your mind is peaceful and content, you contribute to the peacefulness and happiness of the world. You become a wellspring, watering the salt of confusion of everyone around you. Not being self-centered makes you openly compassionate, patient, and understanding. It makes all your relationships easy and natural.

Five Questions to Finding Authentic Happiness

Authentic happiness is founded on the virtues of goodness, truth, and wholesomeness. These virtues are natural to human awareness, to human being. This is what we are born with.

Our inherent virtues are clouded by the demands of existence that lead to the whole realm of desires, then to egotism and injury. It is ignorance of what brings us true happiness that causes us to suffer.

Understanding the true nature of our existence as a pure awareness allows us to free ourselves from ignorance and confusion and find true peace of mind and unconditioned happiness.

Five Questions to Finding Authentic Happiness

Five Questions to Finding Authentic Happiness

Five Questions to Finding Authentic Happiness

www.ingramcontent.com/pod-product-compliance
Lightning Source LLC
Chambersburg PA
CBHW061451040426
42450CB00007B/1312